DACHSHUNDS

BY HEATHER C. MORRIS

Apex is distributed by North Star Editions:
sales@northstareditions.com | 888-417-0195

Produced for Apex by Red Line Editorial.

Photographs ©: Shutterstock Images, cover, 1, 4–5, 6, 7, 9, 12, 13, 14–15, 18–19, 20, 21, 22–23, 25, 26, 27; iStockphoto, 10–11, 16–17, 24, 29

Library of Congress Control Number: 2023921619

ISBN
978-1-63738-906-5 (hardcover)
978-1-63738-946-1 (paperback)
979-8-89250-043-2 (ebook pdf)
979-8-89250-004-3 (hosted ebook)

Printed in the United States of America
Mankato, MN
082024

NOTE TO PARENTS AND EDUCATORS

Apex books are designed to build literacy skills in striving readers. Exciting, high-interest content attracts and holds readers' attention. The text is carefully leveled to allow students to achieve success quickly. Additional features, such as bolded glossary words for difficult terms, help build comprehension.

TABLE OF CONTENTS

CHAPTER 1

EARTHDOG TEST

A dachshund crawls through a dark tunnel. The dog sniffs as he hurries along. He is searching for rats. He follows their scent.

Dachshunds are good at finding animals in dens and tunnels.

The narrow tunnel twists and turns. But the dog's small body fits easily. And his strong sense of smell helps him find the way.

Dachshunds are scent hounds. That means they hunt by smell.

In earthdog events, the animals that dogs try to find are called the quarry.

EARTHDOG EVENTS

Earthdog events test how well dogs track small animals. Each dog must find a cage full of **rodents**. The dog moves through tunnels. Some tunnels have **obstacles**.

At the end of the tunnel, the dachshund finds a cage of rats. The dog barks. He has passed the earthdog test!

FAST FACT

To pass earthdog tests, dogs must "work" the rats. Dogs bark, dig, growl, or bite the cage bars.

Earthdogs may bark or paw at rodents. But the rodents stay safe inside cages.

CHAPTER 2

DACHSHUND HISTORY

Dachshunds come from Germany. Their history goes back more than 300 years. Early dachshunds were hunting dogs. They helped people catch small animals underground.

The dachshund's look has changed over time. Early dachshunds were not as short.

Dachshunds are small but strong. They can move and dig quickly.

At first, these den-hunting dogs came in several sizes. But by the 1800s, the dachshund **breed** had a **distinct** look. This breed spread to England and the United States.

DIGGING IN DENS

Dachshund is German for "badger dog." The dogs often chased badgers into dens. The dogs' big paws helped with digging. And their floppy ears kept out dirt.

Badgers are tough animals. So, dachshunds were bred to be brave.

In 2022, dachshunds were among the 10 most popular dog breeds in the United States.

14

Throughout the 1900s, people continued using dachshunds to hunt. The dogs also became popular pets. Today, many people own them.

FAST FACT

The artist Pablo Picasso had a dachshund named Lump. The dog appears in several of his paintings.

CHAPTER 3

APPEARANCE

Dachshunds are small dogs with long bodies and short legs. They come in two sizes. Miniature dachshunds are tiny. Most weigh less than 11 pounds (5 kg).

Miniature dachshunds stand just 5 to 6 inches (13 to 15 cm) tall.

Standard dachshunds are slightly bigger. They weigh 16 to 32 pounds (7 to 15 kg).

SMALL SIZE, BIG BARK

Despite their small size, dachshunds make good watchdogs. They are brave and smart. And they can bark loudly. They will work hard to **protect** their families.

Standard dachshunds are 8 to 9 inches (20 to 23 cm) tall.

A dachshund's fur can be brown, black, cream, red, or gray.

Dachshunds come in many colors. The breed also has three coat types. Smooth dachshunds have short, shiny fur. Wire-haired dachshunds have short, rough fur. There are also long-haired dachshunds.

FAST FACT

A dachshund's fur can have stripes or patches of color.

A long-haired dachshund's fur is soft and sleek.

CHAPTER 4

CARE AND TRAINING

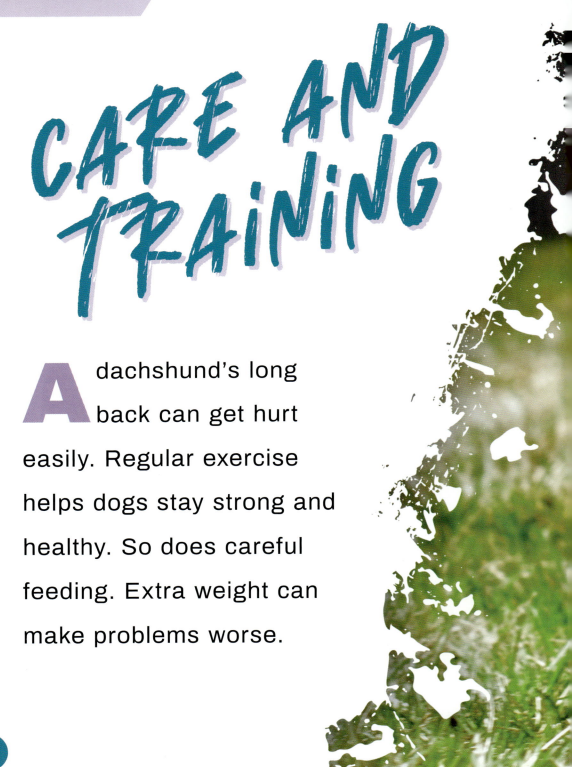

Adachshund's long back can get hurt easily. Regular exercise helps dogs stay strong and healthy. So does careful feeding. Extra weight can make problems worse.

Dachshunds love to run. But owners should not let them jump too high.

Grooming is also important. All dachshunds need regular brushing. Dogs with wire-haired coats need their fur **stripped** as well.

Stripping pulls out the extra fur from dogs with wiry coats.

Dachshunds can be **stubborn**. So, they can be tricky to train. Owners must be patient and **consistent**. They can reward good behavior with treats and praise.

Dachshunds may bark or dig when they are not supposed to.

In agility, the dog that completes the course fastest wins.

DOING AGILITY

Dachshunds can compete in **agility**. In this sport, dogs run through an obstacle course. It has tunnels, ramps, and jumps. Trainers run with their dogs and guide them.

COMPREHENSION QUESTIONS

Write your answers on a separate piece of paper.

1. Write a few sentences describing why people began breeding dachshunds.

2. Would you want to own a dachshund? Why or why not?

3. Which type of dachshund needs its fur stripped?

   A. long-haired

   B. wire-haired

   C. smooth

4. How would having short legs help a dachshund find badgers?

   A. The dog could fit into small tunnels.

   B. The dog could jump high into the air.

   C. The dog could hide in tall grass.

5. What does **scent** mean in this book?

*The dog sniffs as he hurries along. He is searching for rats. He follows their **scent**.*

    A. sound

    B. smell

    C. size

6. What does **reward** mean in this book?

*They can **reward** good behavior with treats and praise.*

    A. give an animal things it likes so it learns how to act

    B. take something away from an animal

    C. get an animal to stop doing something

Answer key on page 32.

29

GLOSSARY

agility
A sport where dogs run through an obstacle course.

breed
A specific type of dog that has its own looks and abilities.

consistent
Done the same way over and over.

distinct
Different from anything else.

obstacles
Things that block the way.

protect
To keep something or someone safe.

rodents
Small, furry animals with large front teeth, such as rats or mice.

stripped
Plucked out extra hairs to help fur stay smooth and healthy.

stubborn
Not willing to change how one thinks or acts.

BOOKS

Green, Sara. *Hounds*. Minneapolis: Bellwether Media, 2021.

Kington, Emily. *Dogs: An Illustrated Guide to 100 Brilliant Breeds*. Truro, UK: Hungry Tomato, 2023.

Norton, Elisabeth. *Sniffer Dogs*. Mendota Heights, MN: Apex Editions, 2023.

ONLINE RESOURCES

Visit **www.apexeditions.com** to find links and resources related to this title.

ABOUT THE AUTHOR

Heather C. Morris writes books for kids who love science and imagination. She lives in the foothills of the Appalachians with her family and their beloved border collie/Great Pyrenees mix. She is secretly in love with her friend's long-haired dachshund named Frodo.

INDEX